Great
SANDWICHES

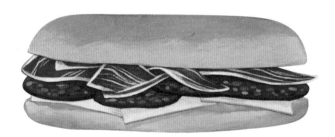

Great SANDWICHES

The world's best combos, from stacks and clubs to melts and subs

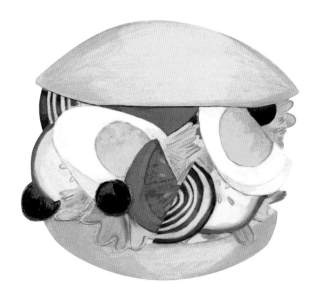

KATHERINE BEBO

DOG 'N' BONE

First published in 2023 by Dog 'n' Bone Books

An imprint of Ryland Peters & Small Ltd.
20–21 Jockey's Fields
London WC1R 4BW
341 E 116th St
New York, NY 10029

www.rylandpeters.com

10 9 8 7 6 5 4 3 2 1

A CIP catalog record for this book is available from
the Library of Congress and the British Library.

ISBN: 978 1 912983 65 0

Printed in China

Art Director: Sally Powell
Designer: Geoff Borin
Senior Editor: Abi Waters
Editorial Director: Julia Charles
Creative Director: Leslie Harrington
Head of Production: Patricia Harrington
Illustrator: Kaitlin Mechan
Indexer: Vanessa Bird

MIX
Paper from
responsible sources
FSC® C106563
FSC
www.fsc.org

CONTENTS

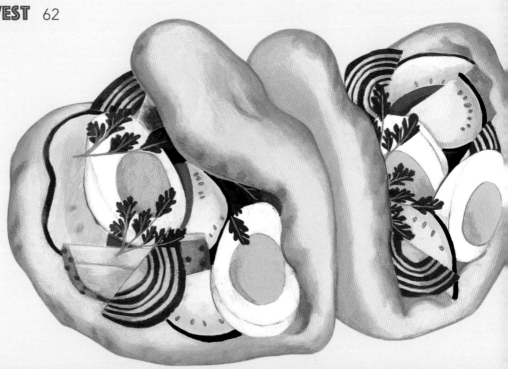

THE BEST THING SINCE
Sliced Bread

Food fads come and go. In the 1970s, fondues and quiches were all the rage; people couldn't get enough kale and quinoa in the 2010s; and anything and everything that could be cooked in an air fryer was the plat du jour in 2023. But the classic sandwich has endured the test of time. Ever since 1762, when John Montagu – the 4th Earl of Sandwich – asked for a serving of roast beef between two slices of bread so he didn't have to interrupt his card playing to go and eat, the world has been relishing sandwiches with glee.

Sandwiches come in many forms: paninis, wraps, pittas, tortillas, rolls, baguettes, bagels, subs, butties, hoagies… With seemingly endless combinations of breads, meats, cheeses, vegetables and spreads, there are more possibilities than you can shake a French stick at. This book has narrowed them down to 50 of the most stand-out servings from around the globe.

The East is East and Go West chapters will take you on a taste-bud-tingling tour of the world – stopping off in Israel to scarf a Sabich and Italy to polish off a Piadina. The selection of Hugs on a Plate are so comforting, as you sink your teeth into them it'll be like sinking into a warm bubble bath. The Go Big or Go Home recipes are as thrilling as they are filling; the Breakfast Feasts serve up a first-thing flavour frenzy; and the Classics will take you on a tasty trip down memory lane. Healthy happiness is on the menu with Live Life on the Veg, while A Different Kettle of Fish invites you to take the plunge into the world of seafood sarnies. Last but by no means least, Summer Treats will bring sunshine to your life – and your plate.

Great Sandwiches offers paninis with panache, buns with bounce and flatbreads with flair. True flour power, whichever way you slice it.

SPREAD THE LOVE

Yes, you can buy these spreads, mayonnaises, dips and sauces ready-made from the supermarket, but homemade is always best. So flick through the recipes in this book and see which sandwiches you might want to jazz up with a little something extra. Then don your apron and hit the kitchen. Each recipe in this section will make far more than you need for one sandwich, so you could either add your creations to many different sandwiches or branch out and use them in other culinary delights – pasta and pesto, anyone?

Basic Pesto

1 large garlic clove, crushed

100 g/3½ oz. pine nuts, toasted

2 bunches fresh basil, stems removed

150 ml/⅔ cup extra virgin olive oil

100 g/3½ oz. Parmesan cheese, finely grated

salt

MAKES ABOUT 300 G/ 1½ CUPS

Place the garlic, pine nuts and basil in a food processor. Keep the motor running and slowly pour in the olive oil. Scrape the mixture into a bowl and stir in the Parmesan and a small pinch of salt.

Pour the pesto into an airtight container. Once sealed the pesto will keep in the fridge for up to 10 days.

Tartare Sauce

225 g/1 cup mayonnaise (see page 8)

80 g/½ cup pickles/gherkins

1 teaspoon capers, chopped

2 teaspoons Dijon mustard

2 teaspoons chopped shallots

2 tablespoons chopped spring onions/scallions

2 teaspoons freshly squeezed lemon juice

salt and freshly ground black pepper

MAKES ABOUT 300 G/ 1½ CUPS

Mix all the ingredients together in a mixing bowl. Store in an airtight container in the fridge for up to 2 days.

Mayonnaise

1 tablespoon Dijon mustard

½ teaspoon salt

½ teaspoon white pepper

2 egg yolks, at room temperature

180 ml/¾ cup grapeseed or sunflower oil

3 tablespoons extra virgin olive oil

1 tablespoon freshly squeezed lemon juice

1 teaspoon caster/superfine sugar

MAKES ABOUT 400 G/ 2 CUPS

In a food processor, pulse the mustard, salt, pepper and egg yolks. With the motor running, slowly drizzle in the oils until they are incorporated. Add the lemon juice and sugar and pulse again. Spoon into an airtight container. Refrigerate for up to 4 days.

VARIATIONS:

Simply stir these extra ingredients into the freshly prepared mayonnaise:

Saffron garlic Add 1 teaspoon crushed saffron threads (soaked in 1 tablespoon hot water) and 1 crushed garlic clove.

Caperberry, chive and onion Add 1 tablespoon each of chopped caperberries, chives and caramelized onion.

Fresh herb Add 3 tablespoons mixed fresh chopped herbs such as tarragon, parsley, basil, coriander/cilantro, chives or dill.

Orange, olive and parsley Add 1 tablespoon finely grated orange zest, 1 tablespoon chopped black olives and 2 tablespoons chopped fresh parsley.

Smoky paprika Add 1 tablespoon sweet Spanish paprika, 1 crushed garlic clove and 1 teaspoon finely grated lemon zest.

Lemon and fennel seed Add the finely grated zest of 1 lemon, 1 tablespoon freshly squeezed lemon juice, 1 teaspoon ground fennel seeds and 1 tablespoon chopped fresh parsley.

Mustard and shallot Add 2 tablespoons grainy mustard, 1 tablespoon Dijon mustard and 1 tablespoon finely chopped shallot.

Black Olive Paste

500 g/1lb 2oz. dry-cured black olives, stoned/pitted

2 tablespoons capers, rinsed

8 canned anchovy fillets, rinsed and chopped

½ teaspoon freshly ground black pepper

1 small hot chilli/chile, finely chopped, or 1 garlic clove, chopped (optional)

1 teaspoon dried oregano, marjoram or thyme

100 ml/scant ½ cup extra virgin olive oil

MAKES ABOUT 500 G/ 2 CUPS

Put the olives in a food processor with the capers, anchovies, pepper, chilli or garlic, if using, and the dried herbs. Chop in several short, pulsing bursts. With the machine running, slowly pour in the oil through the feed tube, until the mixture forms a rich, coarse purée. Don't over-process: some contrast is important.

The paste can be stored in the fridge for up to 2 weeks.

Hummus

1 x 400-g/14-oz can chickpeas/garbanzo beans, drained

freshly squeezed juice of 1 lemon

5 tablespoons light tahini paste

2 tablespoons light olive oil

1 garlic clove, crushed

2 tablespoons boiling water

salt

MAKES ABOUT 400 G/ 2 CUPS

Put the chickpeas and lemon juice in a food processor or blender and work to a smooth purée. Add the tahini paste, olive oil and garlic and blend until smooth. Scrape down the sides of the blender and add the boiling water. The consistency of the mixture should be fairly loose and light. Taste and adjust the seasoning with a little sea salt if necessary. The hummus will keep in the fridge for a couple of days.

CHAPTER 1

CLASSICS

Who doesn't love an oldie but a goodie? With this scrumptious selection of timeless treats, every bite will bring the sweet taste of nostalgia. The PB&J may evoke childhood lunchbox recollections, while the Coronation Chicken Sandwich might transport you back to your auntie's annual garden party. The Roast Beef and Mustard, Pastrami on Rye and Sloppy Joe will offer your red-meat fix, while the Chip Butty will embrace you in a carb-on-carb cuddle.

Pastrami on RYE

Described as 'New York's signature sandwich', the Pastrami on Rye was created by Lithuanian immigrant Sussman Volk in 1888, who owned one of the first delis in NYC. Since then, Katz's Delicatessen has become known as THE PLACE to get your pastrami fix. As well as being famous for its smoky, salty, spicy meat, Katz's has also made a name for itself on the big screen, featuring in many films, including *Donnie Brasco*, *We Own the Night*, *Enchanted* and *When Harry Met Sally* – in the unforgettable 'I'll have what she's having' scene. YES! YES! YES!

225 g/8 oz. pastrami, thinly sliced

2 slices Swiss cheese

2 slices rye bread

1 tablespoon Dijon or yellow mustard

65 g/½ cup coleslaw (optional)

MAKES 1

Place the pastrami in a frying pan/skillet over medium heat. Cook both sides for 2–3 minutes, then add the cheese on top and continue to cook until it's melted.

Meanwhile, toast the bread in a toaster or under the grill/broiler. Spread the mustard evenly on both slices of bread. Place the pastrami and melted cheese on one slice and close the sandwich with the other slice.

If desired, add coleslaw to the sandwich, or serve on the side.

Coronation
CHICKEN SANDWICH

Are you ready to get regal and munch like a monarch? Originally served at the coronation luncheon for Queen Elizabeth II in 1953, coronation chicken maintains its stately esteem today; the crowning glory of any lunchtime. Made with velvety mayonnaise, sweet mango chutney, mild curry powder and plump sultanas, the flavours and textures combine to throw a (garden) party in your mouth like no other. Union Jack bunting optional… but highly recommended.

3 tablespoons mayonnaise (see page 8)

1 tablespoon mango chutney

1½ teaspoons mild curry powder

1 tablespoon sultanas/golden raisins

250 g/9 oz. cooked chicken, shredded

4 slices crusty white bread

butter, at room temperature

handful baby spinach leaves

freshly ground black pepper

MAKES 2

Mix the mayonnaise, mango chutney, curry powder and sultanas together in a bowl. Add the chicken and season with pepper. Stir to coat the chicken. Add a tablespoon of water to loosen, if needed.

Butter 2 slices of bread. Add the spinach and then divide the chicken mixture between the slices. Top with the other 2 bread slices to close, and cut in half or quarters to serve.

Chip BUTTY

Slice some squishy white bread, slather on lashings of butter, and load it up with hot, chunky chips for pure carb-on-carb heaven. The simple chip butty originated in Lancashire in the north of England in the 19th century and has been served in fish and chip shops up and down the country ever since. The classic working-class sandwich has now even been 'gentrified' by Michelin-starred chefs, using triple-cooked chips on toasted sourdough. This comforting doorstep sandwich really is all that and a bag of chips.

3 large floury potatoes, such as Maris Piper, Russet, King Edward or Desirée

2 tablespoons olive oil

1 teaspoon salt

4 slices thick white bread

butter, at room temperature

ketchup (optional)

MAKES 2

Preheat the oven to 200°C/400°F/Gas 6. Peel the potatoes and cut them into chunky chips. Rinse with cold water and pat dry with a paper towel.

Spread the chips on a non-stick baking tray and toss with the olive oil and salt. Arrange them flat in a single layer and roast for 45–50 minutes, turning occasionally, until golden brown and crisp.

Spread a generous layer of butter on 2 slices of bread. Lay the chips on top and squeeze ketchup over, if using. Close with the other bread slices and serve hot.

Sloppy JOE

These days, many an average Joe enjoys this scrummy staple, overflowing with mouthwatering, messy meat – but back in the day, A-listers were the ones getting sloppy. Some say that Sloppy Joe's bar in Havana, Cuba is the birthplace of this sandwich, with the likes of Ernest Hemingway, John Wayne, Clark Gable, Ava Gardner and Frank Sinatra frequenting the joint.

2 tablespoons olive oil

2 garlic cloves, crushed

1 onion, diced

1 celery stalk, finely diced

1 red (bell) pepper, diced

450 g/1 lb. minced/ground beef

2 tablespoons tomato purée/paste

2 tablespoons Worcestershire sauce

2 x 400-gram/14-oz. cans chopped tomatoes

4 burger buns

salt and freshly ground black pepper

SPICE MIX

2 teaspoons smoked paprika

2 teaspoons chilli/chili powder

1 teaspoon celery seeds

1 teaspoon garlic powder

1 teaspoon dried oregano

1 teaspoon English mustard powder

½ teaspoon salt

1 teaspoon ground black pepper

MAKES 4

To make the spice mix, put all the ingredients in a bowl and mix together.

Set a Dutch oven/casserole dish over medium-high heat. Add the oil, garlic and onion and sauté for about 3–5 minutes, until tender and golden brown. Add the celery and pepper and continue to cook for a further 5 minutes until they have taken on some colour.

Add the beef and the prepared spice mix and cook for about 6–8 minutes, until browned, stirring frequently and breaking up any larger pieces.

Stir in the tomato purée, Worcestershire sauce and chopped tomatoes. Season with salt and pepper, then cover the pan and reduce the heat to medium-low. Continue to simmer for 30 minutes, stirring occasionally to stop the mixture sticking to the pan.

Cut the buns in half. Top the bottom halves with generous spoonfuls of the meat mixture. Allow the juices to soak into the bread. Top with the remaining half buns and serve with French fries.

ROAST BEEF
& Mustard Sandwich

Want a classic sandwich that really cuts the mustard? Look no further! The sharp tang of the mustard and horseradish are offset by the cooling sour cream, while the succulent roast beef can be served hot or cold. Either use leftover meat from a roast or beef brisket meal, or high-quality slices from the deli counter. Perfect for those who aren't afraid to take a bite out of life, the bold, beautiful flavours will leave you satisfied… yet hungry for more.

80 g/⅓ cup sour cream

1½ tablespoons Dijon mustard

1½ tablespoons horseradish sauce

8 slices white bread

handful rocket/arugula

16 slices roast beef

salt and freshly ground black pepper

MAKES 4

Combine the sour cream, mustard and horseradish in a bowl and season to taste.

Spread the mixture on 4 slices of bread. Arrange the rocket and roast beef on top. Close each sandwich with the remaining bread and serve.

Peanut Butter & JELLY

PB&J sandwiches are so popular as a lunchbox staple in the United States that the average American will consume almost 3,000 of them throughout their sandwich-chomping lives. Heck, they even celebrate a National Peanut Butter and Jelly Day every year on 2nd April. Other countries are in on the action, too, with Brits replacing the word 'jelly' with 'jam'. Manufacturers have also cottoned on to the taste sensation, producing peanut-butter-and-jelly-flavoured chocolate bars, jelly beans, popcorn, candy floss/cotton candy, coffee and, get this, vodka! If you want to shake things up with a different nut butter, replace the peanuts with Brazil nuts, cashews, almonds, hazelnuts or walnuts. Or try a combination of them all. Go nuts!

2 slices white bread

PEANUT BUTTER

240 g/1¾ cups peanuts

1 teaspoon sugar

1 teaspoon salt

JAM/JELLY

240 g/2½ cup fresh strawberries, finely chopped

freshly squeezed juice of ½ lemon

2 tablespoons sugar

pinch salt

MAKES 1

To make the peanut butter, combine the peanuts, sugar and salt on high speed in a food processor. Pulse for 15–30 seconds (or longer) until the desired smoothness is achieved.

To make the jam, combine the strawberries, lemon juice, sugar and salt in a small saucepan. Cook over low heat for 15–20 minutes until thickened. Remove from the heat and allow to cool.

To make the sandwich, put the slices of bread on a cutting board. On one slice, spread the peanut butter; on the other, spread the jam. Put together to form a sandwich, then cut and serve.

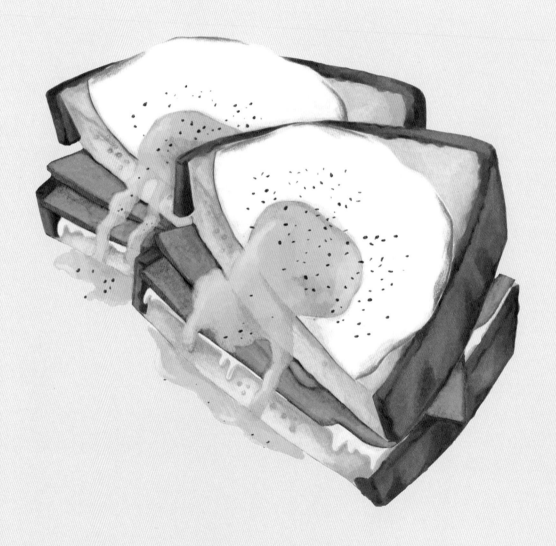

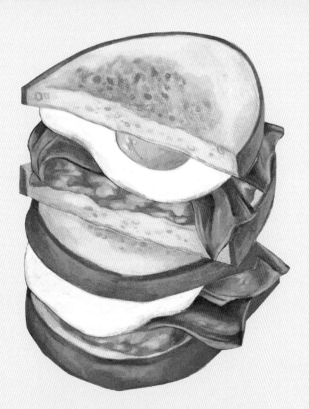

CHAPTER 2

BREAKFAST FEASTS

Start your day with a bang with this selection of spring-out-of-bed sarnies. Go simple with a Fried Egg Sandwich, hipster with Avocado on Toast or 'ooh la la' with a decadent Croque Madame. The Guacamole Breakfast Sandwich and BLT Tortilla Panini use sizzling bacon to ramp things up to next-level luscious. Fuel up and see where the day takes you...

 Avocado TOAST

Scroll through Instagram and it won't be long before you're met with an image of this appetizing open sandwich. Indeed, #avocadotoast has more than 2 million posts… and counting. Create your own Insta-worthy wonder with a few simple smash-hit ingredients. Then, if the mood strikes, raise the stakes with grilled halloumi, poached eggs, toasted pumpkin seeds, balsamic-drizzled tomatoes, pan-fried chickpeas, crumbled feta or, er, steak. Need more inspiration? There are 2 million-plus photos online with your name on. A superfood sandwich with seemingly endless possibilities.

1 ripe avocado

freshly squeezed juice of ½ lemon

pinch chilli flakes/hot red pepper flakes

2 slices sourdough bread

olive oil

salt and freshly ground black pepper

MAKES 2 (SERVES 1)

Cut the avocado in half and remove the stone/pit. Scoop out the flesh and place in a bowl. Add the lemon juice, then mash thoroughly with a fork. Sprinkle in the chilli flakes, then season with salt.

Toast the bread in a toaster or under the grill/broiler. Drizzle over some olive oil, then heap the avocado on top. Grind pepper over and serve.

Fried Egg SANDWICH

A popular British military snack, the Egg Banjo – fried egg sandwich between two thick slices of white bread – got its name because it looks like someone is playing the air banjo when they wipe the spilled yolk from their front, while holding the offending sandwich in the other hand (you're acting it out now, aren't you?). This souped-up – or cheesed-up – version combines crunchy bread, runny yolk and melty cheese to bring music to your lips.

4 slices sourdough bread

Cheddar or Monterey Jack cheese, sliced

1 teaspoon butter

2 large/US extra large eggs

ketchup (optional)

salt and freshly ground black pepper

MAKES 2

Toast the bread in a toaster or under the grill/broiler, then arrange the cheese on all 4 slices. Place under the grill until the cheese melts.

Meanwhile, place the butter in a frying pan/skillet and melt over medium-high heat. Crack the eggs into the pan and cook them how you like.

Remove the cheesy bread from the heat and place one egg on top of a slice, then the other on a different slice. Season. Squeeze ketchup over the eggs, if using. Close the sandwiches, cheese down, with the remaining slices of bread. Serve warm.

Croque MADAME

Well, if this isn't one of the most delicious sandwiches you'll ever taste, you have permission to eat your hat! Which, actually, is kind of what you'll do once you tuck in. A fried egg placed on top of the Croque Monsieur transforms the sandwich into a Croque Madame, and is said to relate to a woman's wide-brimmed hat. Adding to the rich, cheesy family, a Croque Mademoiselle is a vegetarian version, which shuns the egg and replaces the ham with cucumber or zucchini/courgette and herbs. Bon appétit!

4 slices sourdough or crusty white bread

2 teaspoons Dijon mustard

85 g/3 oz. ham

115 g/4 oz. Gruyère cheese, grated

butter, at room temperature

olive oil

2 eggs

freshly ground black pepper

MAKES 2

Spread 2 slices of bread with mustard, then add the ham and half the cheese. Place under the grill/broiler and heat until the cheese is just starting to melt. Top with the remaining slices of bread.

Lightly butter the sandwiches on both sides, then return them to the grill. Grill/broil until golden, then turn over and grill until just golden on the second side. Sprinkle with the remaining cheese and grill for 1 minute, or until the cheese is melted and bubbling.

Heat a little olive oil in a non-stick frying pan/skillet over medium-high heat. Crack the eggs in and fry for around 3 minutes, until the whites are set. Top each sandwich with an egg and grind some black pepper over to serve.

BLT *Tortilla Panini*

In 2014, a record was set for the world's largest Bacon, Lettuce and Tomato Sandwich. Measuring more than 227 feet, it contained 2,000 slices of bacon. While the sandwich constructors were at it, they also set the record for the biggest group of people to perform the #bacondance, which saw 161 individuals 'sizzling' on the floor. While we're not suggesting you attempt creating such a Blooming Long Treat (or rolling around on the ground), we do recommend you Bite (the tortilla), Lick (your lips) and Taste (the fine flavour) of this BLT with a difference.

16 slices bacon

4 large flour tortillas

4 ripe tomatoes, sliced

115 g/4 oz. Gruyère cheese, sliced

250 g/2 cups shredded crisp lettuce

60 g/¼ cup mayonnaise (see page 8)

salt and freshly ground black pepper

MAKES 4

Place the bacon in a frying pan/skillet over medium heat and cook gently until brown and crisp.

Put the tortillas on a work surface and arrange 4 bacon slices down the centre of each one. Top with the tomato slices, cheese, lettuce and mayonnaise, then lightly sprinkle with salt and pepper.

Fold the edges over to form a wrap and cook seam-side down in a hot stove-top grill pan for 2 minutes. Flip and cook for a further 2 minutes on the second side. Serve hot.

GUACAMOLE
Breakfast Sandwich

This creamy, crispy, crunchy creation will guac your world. They say breakfast is the most important meal of the day; with this protein-packed pow-on-a-plate, it can also be the most delicious. It sure beats muesli! Add tomatoes, cheese, Tabasco sauce or anything else your tingling taste buds might desire. Ripe – but not bruised – avocados are essential to ensure the perfect taste and consistency of the gorgeous green stuff. Holy guacamole!

4 slices sourdough bread

butter, at room temperature

olive oil

4 slices bacon

2 eggs

GUACAMOLE

1½ very ripe avocados

½ large tomato, very finely diced

freshly squeezed juice of ½ large lime

handful fresh coriander/ cilantro, finely chopped

½ small red onion, finely chopped

½ red or green chilli/ chile, deseeded and finely chopped

salt and freshly ground black pepper

MAKES 2

To make the guacamole, halve and stone/pit the avocados and scoop the flesh into a bowl. Add the tomato. Tip the lime juice, coriander, red onion and chilli into the bowl, then season. Use a fork to mash all the ingredients together.

Toast the bread in a toaster or under a grill/broiler.

Meanwhile, heat a little olive oil in a pan and fry the bacon until slightly crispy, and the eggs until the white is set but the yolk is still runny.

Butter the toast, then divide the guacamole between 2 slices (if there's too much, save some to serve on the side). Add 2 slices of bacon to each slice, then 1 egg on top. Close with the other bread slices and cut in half. Serve immediately.

CHAPTER 3

A HUG ON A PLATE

Is there anything more cosily comforting than oozing, melted cheese; thick, sweet chocolate spread; hot, sauce-covered meatballs? Not in the same dish, obviously. Indulging in the sandwiches in this chapter is like being enveloped in a giant, fleecy blanket with bunny rabbits on. So ease yourself into your fluffy slippers and prepare for a feast of Mozzarella in Carozza, Welsh Rarebit, Nutella and Banana on Brioche… and more. Is it nap time yet?

The REUBEN

Ladies and gentlemen, I present to you… drum roll please… the award-winning Reuben! Get your laughing gear round this corned beef, provolone cheese, Russian dressing and sauerkraut sandwich and you'll see why it won the National Sandwich Idea Contest in 1956, held in Omaha, Nebraska. The judges called it a 'hearty man-sized sandwich'. Since then, it's become particularly popular in American Jewish-style delis, even though it's technically not kosher as it combines meat with cheese.

RUSSIAN DRESSING

340 g/1½ cups mayonnaise (see page 8)

150 ml/⅔ cup chilli/chile sauce

75 g/⅓ cup sour cream

2 tablespoons horseradish sauce

1 tablespoon freshly squeezed lemon juice

2 teaspoons caster/superfine sugar

2 teaspoons Worcestershire sauce

½ teaspoon hot sauce

½ teaspoon paprika

1 dill pickle, chopped

1 spring onion/scallion, chopped

SANDWICHES

225 g/1⅓ cup sauerkraut, drained and squeezed of moisture

8 slices rye bread

8–16 slices provolone cheese

450 g/1 lb. corned beef, sliced

butter, at room temperature

salt and freshly ground black pepper

fries, to serve (optional)

MAKES 4

To make the Russian dressing, mix all the ingredients in a food processor until combined. Season with salt and pepper to taste. Refrigerate.

Build the sandwich: mix half of the Russian dressing with the sauerkraut. Lay 4 slices of rye bread down and place 1–2 slices of provolone cheese on each one, followed by a generous serving of corned beef and another 1–2 slices of cheese. Top with the sauerkraut mixture and a second piece of bread. Butter the outside of the sandwiches.

Heat a ridged griddle/grill pan over low-medium heat. Add the sandwiches and cook for 2–3 minutes per side until the cheese has melted. Serve with fries, if you like, and extra Russian dressing on the side.

Welsh RAREBIT

It's said that the seriously satisfying Welsh Rarebit can cause vivid dreams. Indeed, a 1902 book entitled *Welsh Rarebit Tales* is a collection of short stories – horror, sci-fi, dark crime – written by members of a writing club who ate the cheesy dish before bedtime. Certainly, the combination of crunchy bread, sharp Cheddar, bitter ale and warming mustard – complemented by a Worcestershire sauce kick – is both deliciously dreamy and scarily scrumptious. Night-night!

2 slices ciabatta or sourdough bread

30 g/2 tablespoons unsalted butter, plus extra for spreading

30 g/3 tablespoons plain/all-purpose flour

125 ml/½ cup ale, at room temperature

1 teaspoon mustard powder

150 g/5 oz. mature/sharp Cheddar cheese, grated

1 tablespoon Worcestershire sauce

pinch ground cayenne pepper

MAKES 2

Butter the bread slices on one side. In a small saucepan over low heat, combine the butter and flour, stirring until melted. Pour the ale in gradually and stir continuously until the mixture thickens. Add the mustard powder, cheese, Worcestershire sauce and cayenne pepper, and stir to just melt the cheese before taking the pan off the heat.

Put the slices of bread, butter-side up, under the grill/broiler and heat until golden brown. Flip the slices over and top with the cheese mixture. Grill/broil for 1–2 minutes, until bubbling. Leave to cool for a minute or two before serving.

Meatball SUB

Goodness gracious, great balls of flavour! Delve deep into this Italian-American meatball sub and submerge yourself in a taste explosion. You'll not want to come up for air as you navigate your way through the juicy meatballs, thick marinara sauce and gooey cheese. Abbreviated from 'submarine' due to its shape resembling the underwater craft, depending on where you're from, you may actually know such bread rolls as grinders, torpedoes, heroes, hoagies, wedges or spuckies. Call them what you will, but definitely call them yummy.

2 submarine rolls

olive oil

4–6 slices Fontina cheese or about 250 g/3 cups grated

MEATBALLS

225 g/8 oz. minced/ground meat, half beef and half Italian sausage (or pork)

30 g/½ cup fresh breadcrumbs

1 teaspoon dried oregano

1 teaspoon dried rosemary

pinch chilli flakes/hot red pepper flakes, or more to taste

1 egg, beaten

2 tablespoons milk, or more if necessary

1 teaspoon salt

TOMATO/MARINARA SAUCE

3 garlic cloves, crushed but not peeled

olive oil

15 g/1 tablespoon unsalted butter

200 g/7 oz. passata/strained tomatoes

pinch caster/granulated sugar

salt and freshly ground black pepper

baking sheet, lined with parchment paper

MAKES 2

Preheat the oven to 190°C/375°F/Gas 5.

In a bowl, combine all the meatball ingredients and mix well. The mixture should be firm enough to form into balls but moist enough so they are not dry; add more milk as required. Form them into 8–10 golf-ball-sized balls and arrange on the baking sheet. Bake until browned and cooked though; about20–30 minutes. Remove from the oven and allow the meatballs to cool slightly.

Meanwhile, prepare the sauce. Coat the garlic cloves lightly with oil, place in a small ovenproof dish such as a ramekin and roast, at the same time as the meatballs, for 10–15 minutes until golden and tender. Be careful not to let the garlic burn. Remove the garlic from the oven, slip the cloves from their skins and chop finely. In a small saucepan, melt the butter. Add the passata, garlic, sugar, salt and pepper. Simmer for 15 minutes, then taste and adjust the seasoning, and keep warm until needed.

Cut the submarine rolls in half lengthways. Brush olive oil over the bread and place under the grill/broiler until lightly toasted. Arrange 4–5 meatballs inside each sub and coat with the tomato sauce. Place the cheese on top, and place back under the grill until the cheese has melted. Serve hot.

MOZZARELLA
in Carrozza

Saddle up for a serious taste sensation. Basically a mozzarella stick in sandwich form, you might choose to serve this Italian stallion of a snack alongside marinara sauce or pesto for dipping. In parts of Italy, you may also find prosciutto, 'nduja or anchovies inside. For ultimate sandwich success, opt for low-moisture mozzarella, rather than the type sold in liquid. Translated, it's called 'mozzarella in carriage' because when pulled apart, the cheese strings are said to resemble the reins of a horse and carriage. Giddy up!

4 large slices coarse, country-style Italian bread, such as Pugliese

125 g/4½ oz. mozzarella cheese, thinly sliced

125 ml/½ cup milk

2 eggs

virgin olive oil, for frying

salt and freshly ground black pepper (optional)

MAKES 2

Put the slices of bread onto a board. Arrange the sliced mozzarella over 2 of the slices. Season with pepper, if using. Put the other slices of bread on top.

Put the milk and eggs into a shallow dish, season with a pinch of salt and whisk well.

Pour about 2 cm/¾ in. depth of the virgin olive oil into a large, heavy-based frying pan/skillet. Heat to 190°C/375°F or until a small cube of bread turns golden brown in about 40 seconds. Have a spatula or slotted spoon ready.

Dip the sandwiches into the egg mixture until thoroughly wet.

Using the spatula or slotted spoon, slide both sandwiches into the hot oil and fry for about 4–5 minutes, turning them over carefully, once, using tongs.

Remove from the oil with the tongs or a slotted spoon, then drain on paper towels. Serve whole or sliced into pieces; eat them hot.

Croque MONSIEUR

Get your 'Chomps-Élysées' on with this fabulous French dish, consisting of magnificently melted cheese and ham – plus béchamel sauce for a little *je ne sais quoi*. The Brits may be so unimaginative as to call this sandwich a cheese and ham toastie, whereas Americans have the exciting-sounding Monte Cristo, which is a slight variation in that the sandwich is dipped in egg before being toasted/pan-fried. Translated, the name comes from the French words *croque* (meaning 'crunch') and *monsieur* (meaning 'mister'). It's crunch time, people!

4 slices sourdough or crusty white bread

115 g/4 oz. Gruyère cheese, grated

85 g/3 oz. ham

butter, at room temperature

BÉCHAMEL SAUCE

125ml/½ cup milk

125ml½ cup cream

1 garlic clove, crushed

2 bay leaves

1 small onion, chopped

20 g/1½ tablespoons butter

20 g/2 tablespoons plain/ all-purpose flour

1 heaped teaspoon Dijon mustard

fresh nutmeg, grated

salt and freshly ground black pepper

MAKES 2

To make the béchamel sauce, stir the milk, cream, garlic, bay leaves and onion together in a small pan over medium heat. When nearly boiling, turn the heat off and leave for 10 minutes to blend the flavours. Pour the liquid through a sieve/strainer and discard the bay leaves and onion.

Melt the butter in another pan, then add the flour and cook over gentle heat for 1–2 minutes. Whisk in the warm milk mixture gradually and bring to a gentle boil, stirring regularly. Add the mustard, a little grating of fresh nutmeg and some salt and pepper.

Spread 2 slices of bread with some béchamel sauce. Add the ham and half the cheese. Place under the grill/broiler and heat until the cheese is just starting to melt. Top with the remaining slices of bread.

Lightly butter the sandwiches on both sides, then return them to the grill. Grill/broil until golden, then carefully turn over and grill until just golden on the second side. Sprinkle with the remaining cheese and grill for 1 minute, or until the cheese is melted and bubbling. Grind some black pepper over them to serve, along with any leftover béchamel sauce on the side.

Nutella & Banana
ON BRIOCHE

Is there anything more deliciously decadent than dipping your spoon in and devouring Nutella straight from the jar? Indeed, this chocolate-hazelnut spread sure knows how to spread some joy. Take things to the next level by adding bread and banana to the mix. Not only will this delectable sandwich melt in your mouth, you'll feel positively virtuous (maybe) as the banana counts as one of your five a day. High five!

4 thick slices brioche bread

4 tablespoons Nutella or other chocolate-hazelnut spread

1 small banana, thinly sliced

vegetable oil

MAKES 2

Preheat a panini grill. Spread 2 slices of the brioche with Nutella. Place the banana slices on top. Close the sandwiches with the second slice of brioche.

Brush both sides of the panini press with a little oil and heat the brioche for around 2 minutes until the bread is golden brown and the filling warmed through.

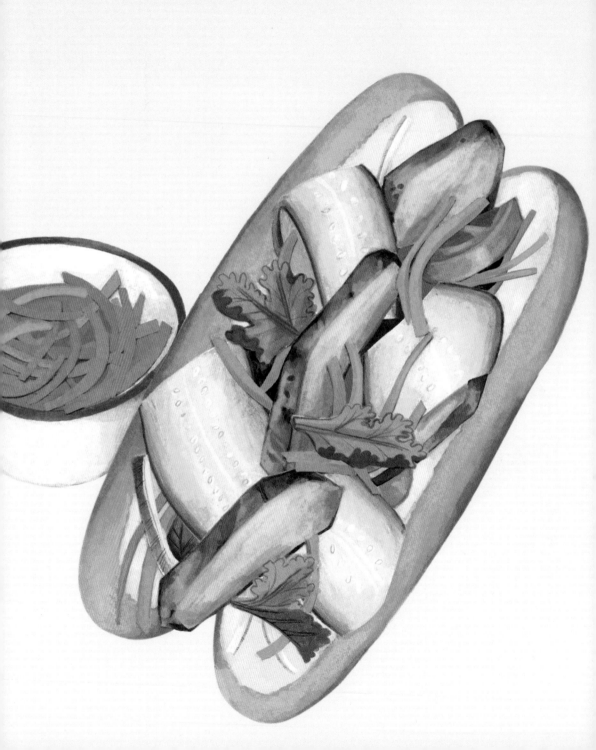

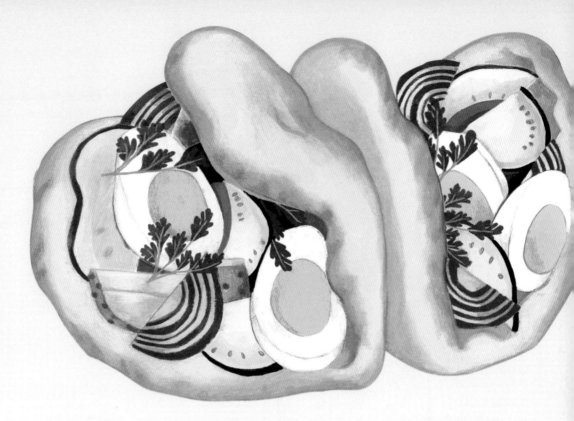

CHAPTER 4

EAST IS EAST

Are you ready for a truly appetizing adventure? Navigate and nibble your way around the Eastern part of the world, stopping off in Japan, Vietnam, Lebanon and Israel. Excite and delight your taste buds with aromatic herbs, spices, zests and tangs – savouring the exotic with Bánh Mì, Man'oushe, Katsu Sando and Sabich. A beast of a feast from the East.

Katsu SANDO

This jaunty Japanese sandwich is a cutlet above the rest! Breaded and fried, the crispy, tender meat is complemented perfectly by a generous slathering of tasty tonkatsu sauce and the crunch of marinated cabbage. The traditional Japanese condiments Karashi mustard and Kewpie mayonnaise are ideal, but if you're not able to find them, the suggested substitutes still work.

¼ small white cabbage, finely shredded

½ tablespoon rice wine vinegar

100 g/3½ oz. panko breadcrumbs

2 pork escalopes or chicken breast fillets, bashed flat

2 tablespoons plain/all-purpose flour

1 egg, beaten

vegetable oil, for frying

4 slices thick white bread

Karashi/Japanese or Dijon mustard

Kewpie or regular mayonnaise

salt and freshly ground black pepper

TONKATSU SAUCE

3 tablespoons Worcestershire sauce

4 tablespoons ketchup

¼ teaspoon English mustard powder

1½ teaspoons soy sauce

¼ teaspoon garlic powder

MAKES 2

Mix all the tonkatsu sauce ingredients together and set aside. Put the cabbage in a small bowl and pour the rice wine vinegar over the top. Leave to marinate.

Season the breadcrumbs with salt and pepper and spread out on a plate. Coat the pork or chicken in flour, dip into the egg, then into the breadcrumbs, completely coating the meat.

In a thick frying pan/skillet, heat 2.5 cm/1 in. of oil. Fry the cutlets one at a time, turning frequently, until browned and cooked through. Remove from the pan and place on paper towels to soak up any excess oil.

Cut the crusts off the bread and spread 2 pieces with a thin layer of mustard, then a generous layer of mayonnaise. Chop each cutlet in half and place on top of the bread slices. Top with the tonkatsu sauce, followed by some cabbage. Close with the remaining slices of bread, cut in half and serve.

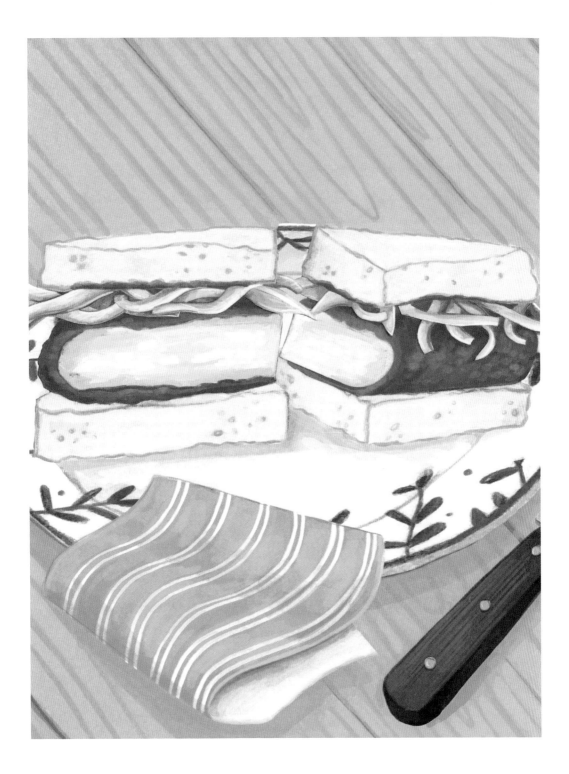

Chicken SHAWARMA

Tender, tantalizing and terrifically tasty, this Middle Eastern dish will send your taste buds into a spin. The chicken is traditionally cooked on a rotating spit, but presumably you haven't decked your kitchen out like a kebab shop (imagine!), so you'll have to prepare the chicken in your boring old (non-rotating) oven. But don't worry – with the zingy, zesty, zippy marinade, the flavour is the exact opposite of boring. Serve drizzled with tahini, hummus or garlic sauce for added pizzazz.

150 g/⅔ cup natural yogurt

freshly squeezed juice of 1 lemon

4 garlic cloves, crushed

1 green chilli/chile

thumb-sized piece ginger, grated

handful fresh coriander/cilantro, chopped

1 teaspoon garam masala

1 teaspoon ground cumin

½ teaspoon turmeric

1 teaspoon salt

16 boneless, skinless chicken thighs

6 laffa, naan or other flatbreads

tomatoes, sliced

cucumber, sliced

pickles, sliced

onion, sliced

tahini, hummus or garlic sauce (optional)

2 long metal skewers

MAKES 6

Tip the yogurt, lemon juice, garlic, chilli, ginger, fresh coriander, spices and salt into a blender and whizz up. Put the chicken into a large bowl or container, pour over the mixture, ensuring the chicken is completely coated. Cover and marinate for at least 4 hours – overnight would be better.

Preheat the oven to 200°C/400°F/Gas 6. Thread the chicken onto the metal skewers (so that both skewers go through each piece of meat). Suspend this over a roasting pan or, if it's not long enough, place a wire rack over a roasting pan and sit the chicken on top. Bake for around 45–50 minutes until cooked through. Rest for 5 minutes, then carve.

Warm the bread in the oven for a few minutes. Place the chicken on the bread, along with the salad bits. Drizzle over some tahini, hummus or garlic sauce, if using. Fold in half and serve.

SABICH

How do you like your eggs? How about hard-boiled, then layered with fried slices of aubergine/eggplant, tahini, tomato, cucumber, cabbage, hummus and mmm-mmm mango sauce, all squeezed inside a pitta bread? Some versions even find room for boiled potatoes, too. Traditionally, this Israeli sandwich – with Iraqi roots – was made with haminados eggs, braised for many hours until the shells turned brown, and laffa bread, which is nicknamed Iraqi pitta. If you'd rather a sabich salad, simply forgo the bread. Cracking stuff.

½ aubergine/eggplant, sliced into 1 cm/½ in. thick rounds

1 teaspoon olive oil

¼ cucumber, chopped

1 tomato, chopped

1 tablespoon fresh flat-leaf parsley, finely chopped

freshly squeezed juice of ½ lemon

3 red cabbage leaves, chopped

1 tablespoon white or red wine vinegar

3 tablespoons plain yogurt

3 tablespoons tahini

2 large pitta breads or other flatbreads

2 tablespoons hummus

2 hard-boiled eggs, peeled and sliced

salt and freshly ground black pepper

AMBA SAUCE (OPTIONAL)

1 mango, peeled and stoned/pitted

grated zest and freshly squeezed juice of 2 small limes

½ tablespoon olive oil

1 garlic clove, crushed

¼ teaspoon fenugreek seeds

¼ teaspoon mustard seeds

¼ teaspoon ground turmeric

¼ teaspoon ground cayenne pepper

¼ teaspoon sweet smoked paprika

MAKES 2

Heat a frying pan/skillet over medium-high heat. Brush the aubergine slices with olive oil and fry on both sides, until tender and golden brown. Sprinkle with salt and set aside.

Mix the cucumber, tomatoes, parsley and 1 teaspoon of lemon juice in a bowl. Season to taste and set aside. In a different bowl, toss the cabbage with the vinegar and season with salt. Set aside.

In another bowl, stir the yogurt with the tahini until smooth. Add 1 tablespoon water and the remaining lemon juice. Stir and add salt to taste. Set aside.

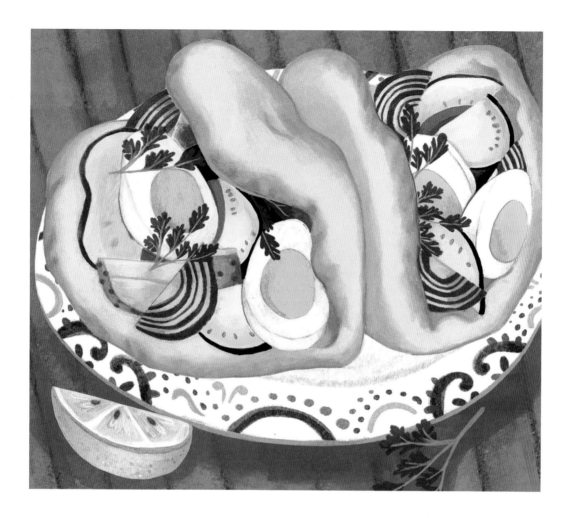

In a toaster, warm the pitta bread, then carefully cut it open to create a pocket. Spread the hummus inside. Place the fried aubergine on top and drizzle with the tahini sauce, then add the sliced eggs, pickled cabbage and cucumber mixture.

You can serve the sandwich now, but if you want to take it to the next level, whip up some amba sauce. Chop the mango and put it into a blender with the lime zest and juice. Whizz until smooth. In a frying pan, place the olive oil, garlic and all the spices, and cook over medium heat. Fry until lightly golden, then stir in the mango. Season, then leave to cool. Drizzle over the pittas or serve on the side.

BÁNH MÌ

Gooooood morning, Vietnaaaaam! Like the rambunctious radio DJ played by Robin Williams in the 1987 film, this 'Saigon sandwich' has stacks of personality. The perfect combination of sweet, sour and spicy, the Bánh Mì is a staple street food in Vietnam. It was immortalized as a food Google Doodle (or 'Foodle') on 24 March 2020, which celebrated its smorgasbord of flavours with a cute animation. On the same day in 2011, 'Bánh Mì' was admitted into the Oxford English Dictionary. Which is really something worth broadcasting.

LEMONGRASS BEEF

100 g/3½ oz. beef, thinly sliced

1 lemongrass stalk, finely chopped

1 garlic clove, finely chopped

1 shallot, finely chopped

1 teaspoon Maggi Seasoning (or soy sauce)

1 teaspoon pork, chicken or vegetable stock

1 teaspoon sugar

PICKLE

2 carrots, shredded

½ daikon/mooli, shredded (optional)

5 tablespoons cider vinegar

5 tablespoons sugar

TO FILL

1 Vietnamese baguette or freshly baked small French baguette

butter, at room temperature or soft cheese

pork or chicken liver pâté

chả chiên Vietnamese ham, thinly sliced

fresh coriander/cilantro (optional)

cucumber, cut into 10-cm/4-in. slivers

spring onions/scallions, thinly sliced lengthways

bird's eye chillies/chiles, thinly sliced

Maggi Seasoning

sriracha chilli/chili sauce (optional)

MAKES 1

Preheat the oven to 220°C/425°F/Gas 7. Mix all the ingredients for the lemongrass beef in a bowl and leave to marinate for 10 minutes. Transfer to a roasting pan and bake in the preheated oven for 15 minutes.

Mix all the ingredients for the pickle in a bowl and allow to rest for 15 minutes. Drain and wring with your hands.

Slit the baguette lengthways and pull out the soft dough inside (which can be used for breadcrumbs). Spread with butter or soft cheese and a smear of pâté. Layer the warm beef and its juices, pickle, ham, coriander, cucumber, spring onions and chillies over the top, then pour over a few drops of Maggi Seasoning and chilli sauce, if using.

MAN'OUSHE

This Lebanese flatbread goes by many (similar) names – manaqish, manaeesh, manakeesh, manooshe, mankousheh, man'oushe – but always rises to the occasion. Vivacious and versatile, its fillings can be creatively customized to suit your mood/what's in your fridge. Offerings including the aromatic herb-and-spice mix zaatar go down a treat, just as something sweet – like chocolate spread and sliced strawberries – do.

500 g/generous 3½ cups strong white bread flour, plus extra for dusting

25 g/2 tablespoons caster/superfine sugar

10 g/¼ oz. instant/fast-action dried yeast

10 g/2 teaspoons salt

20 ml/4 teaspoons olive oil, plus extra for kneading

360 ml/1½ cups lukewarm water

FILLING

1½ tablespoons zaatar seasoning

1 tablespoon olive oil

250 g/9 oz. halloumi

2 large tomatoes, sliced

handful mint leaves

3 baking sheets, lined with baking parchment

MAKES 3

To make the flatbread, combine the flour, sugar, yeast and salt. Add the olive oil and 270 ml/scant 1¼ cups of the water. Mix together using your fingers. Gradually add the rest of the water until you have a soft (not sticky) dough, and all the flour has come away from the sides of the bowl. Note, you may not need all of the water.

Pour a little oil onto a clean worktop and place the dough on top. Knead for 5–10 minutes until smooth. Oil a bowl and place the dough inside. Cover and leave until it has doubled in size, about 1½ hours.

Oil a work surface and place the dough onto it. Knock excess air out of the dough by folding it in on itself. Repeat until the dough is smooth and all the air has been knocked out. Sprinkle a little flour onto a work surface. Split the dough into three, then roll into large circles using a rolling pin.

Preheat the oven to 230°C/450°F/Gas 8. Place one circle of dough on each lined baking sheet and cover with a plastic bag or clean, damp tea towel/dish towel for 20 minutes.

Stir the zaatar and olive oil together. Brush onto the flatbreads and place in the oven for about 15 minutes. Remove the bread from the oven and allow to cool on a wire rack for a few minutes.

Heat the olive oil in a pan and fry the halloumi on both sides until golden brown. Arrange the halloumi, tomato slices and mint leaves on top of each man'oushe. Fold in half and serve.

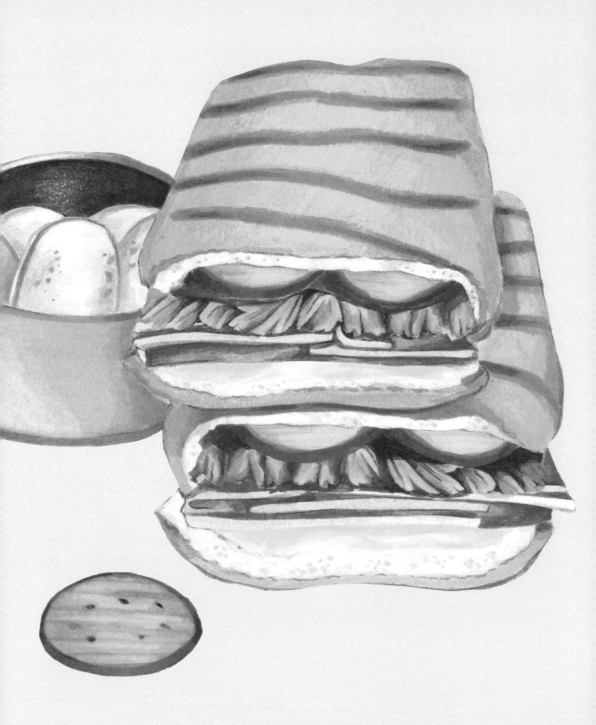

CHAPTER 5

GO WEST

Grab your passport; this chapter will take you to Italy, Spain, France, Cuba and America. On your unforgettable sojourn around the Western world, you'll gorge on gastronomic delights such as Piadina, Jambon-Beurre, Philly Cheesesteak and Bocadillo de Carne y Queso. Every mouthful will take you on a journey of pure joy.

PIADINA

The beauty of this hot little number is that you can fill it with whatever your heart (or stomach) desires. Popular choices include combinations of Italy's heavenly cured meats and cheeses, and a sprinkling of greenery such as rocket/arugula or basil. One may be forgiven for calling it an 'Italian quesadilla' but a Piadina flatbread is actually crumblier than the doughy tortilla. Team with a dry, sparkling Lambrusco to complement the rich, salty flavours. Salute!

2 piadine (or flour tortillas)

250 g/9 oz. bresaola, thinly sliced

Parmigiano Reggiano, sliced as desired

handful rocket/arugula leaves

2–3 tablespoons extra virgin olive oil

freshly ground black pepper

MAKES 2

Lay the piadine on a clean work surface and cover with bresaola. Layer with the cheese and rocket, then season generously with black pepper. Fold in half.

Heat the oil in a frying pan/skillet and fry the piadine for 3 minutes or so on each side until golden. Serve immediately.

FRENCH DIP *Sandwich*

Much like French fries, French dressing and French kissing, the origin of the French Dip Sandwich actually lies outside of France. This succulent sandwich – served with a side of jus for dipping – is an American invention, with the name seemingly referring to the type of bread used. The circumstances of this steaming sandwich's inception have been hotly debated, with one account stating that a chef dipped the sandwich in meat drippings after a customer complained the bread was stale. If eaten correctly, the jus will run down your chin; napkins at the ready.

2 boneless ribeye steaks

1 tablespoon olive oil

1 tablespoon salt

2 teaspoons freshly ground black pepper

1 teaspoon dried sage

2 teaspoons dried oregano

2 hoagie rolls or small French baguettes

4 slices provolone cheese

JUS

¼ onion, thinly sliced

2 teaspoons fresh thyme, chopped

2 garlic cloves, crushed

355ml/1½ cups beef broth or stock

2 teaspoons Worcestershire sauce

MAKES 2

Preheat oven to 230°C/450°F/Gas 8. Rub the steaks with the olive oil and place in a roasting pan. In a bowl, stir together the salt and pepper and herbs. Rub this mix all over the beef. Roast for about 20 minutes. Place on a chopping board to rest and turn the oven down to 180°C/350°F/Gas 4.

To make the jus, place the roasting pan – with beef drippings – on the hob/stovetop and turn to medium heat. Add the onion and cook for about 3 minutes until soft. Add the thyme and garlic and cook for about 1 minute. Add the beef broth and Worcestershire sauce and bring to the boil. Simmer for 8–10 minutes until slightly thickened.

When ready to serve, slice the beef thinly. Fill the rolls with beef and top with provolone cheese. Bake for 10 minutes until the cheese has melted.

Serve with the jus on the side for dipping.

BOCADILLO
de Carne y Queso

Doesn't 'Bocadillo de Carne y Queso' sound so much more exciting, so much more appetizing, so much more sexy than 'Meat and Cheese Sandwich'? But, then, the Spaniards do exciting, appetizing and sexy very well. Almost any meat and cheese goes for the filling – beef, pork, chicken, veal, cured meats… Edam, Gouda, mozzarella, Parmesan, manchego… The key is simplicity; choose good-quality ingredients and you can't go wrong. Go all-out Spanish and serve with patatas bravas, washed down with a glass of fruity Sangria. Then treat yourself to a siesta. Olé!

1 small baguette

1 tablespoon aioli

4 slices manchego cheese

10 pieces dried chorizo, cut into rounds

4 slices Serrano or Iberico ham

MAKES 1

Slice the baguette in half. Spread the aioli evenly across the bottom piece. Place the cheese on top, then add the meat. Close with the top slice of baguette.

CUBAN *Sandwich*

Rum… Cigars… Che Guevara… Three things Cuba is famous for. Add to the list the Cuban Sandwich, otherwise known as the Cubano, a cheese and ham creation with a difference. Layering two types of pig – ham and roast pork – it's every pork-lover's dream. *Oink, oink!* A similar offering is the Medianoche ('Midnight') Sandwich, which began as a late-night snack in the nightclubs of Havana. Containing the same ingredients as a Cuban Sandwich, it's smaller and served on bread similar to challah, rather than crusty Cuban bread.

2 sticks of Cuban bread, or soft baguettes/subs, split in half horizontally

2 teaspoons American mustard (or mild Dijon mustard)

4 slices Emmental

4 slices roast ham

150 g/5½ oz. cooked pork shoulder, thinly sliced or shredded

1–2 gherkins, thinly sliced

knob/pat of butter

MAKES 2

Spread each roll with a spoonful of mustard. Lay the slices of cheese on the bottom, then top with the ham. Add the pork and gherkins.

Heat a ridged griddle/grill pan or frying pan/skillet over medium heat. Melt the butter in the pan, and use it to brush the outside of the sandwiches. Lay the sandwiches in the hot frying pan. Use something heavy – like a cast-iron pot or a baking tray weighed down with cans – to compress the sandwiches.

Cook for 5 minutes before flipping the sandwiches over and repeating the process on the other side. Cook until the ham is hot through and the cheese has melted.

JAMBON *Buerre*

With only three ingredients in this classic French baguette, it's a ménage à trois that will certainly make your mouth water. An absolute favourite in bistros, cafes and brasseries, three million Jambon-Beurres are sold every day in France. Impressive, n'est-ce pas? The epitome of scrumptious simplicity, quality ingredients are an absolute must. Ideally, the ham should be Jambon de Paris but, failing that, go for any ham par excellence. Pure joie de vivre on a plate.

small French baguette

salted butter, at room temperature

3 slices ham

MAKES 1

Cut the baguette in half lengthways. Spread the butter generously, then add the ham.

PHILLY *Cheesesteak*

The city of Philadelphia is home to fictitious boxing legend Rocky Balboa. It's also home to the Philly Cheesesteak, a juicy sandwich that packs a piquant punch. The key to succulent success is paper-thin steak, so make sure to use a sharp knife to slice it. After you've constructed your cheesesteak, why not settle down for a *Rocky* marathon!

2 large onions, thinly sliced

15 g/1 tablespoon unsalted butter

3 tablespoons vegetable oil, plus extra for brushing

350 g/12½ oz. minute/cube steak, thinly sliced

1 ciabatta

2 tablespoons spreadable processed cheese, such as Dairylea or Kraft

6–8 slices Emmental/Swiss cheese

salt and freshly ground black pepper

MAKES 1 (SERVES 2)

In a frying pan/skillet, combine the onions with the butter and 2 tablespoons of the vegetable oil. Cook over medium heat, stirring occasionally, until deep golden brown, for about 10 minutes. Season lightly and transfer to a small bowl.

In the same pan/skillet, add another tablespoon of oil and heat. When hot but not smoking, add the beef and cook for 2–3 minutes, stirring often until cooked through. Season lightly and set aside.

To assemble, slice the ciabatta in half lengthways. Spread the inside of the bottom slice with the processed cheese. With a small brush, coat the outsides of the bread lightly, on both sides, with oil.

Assemble just before cooking, in a large, heavy-based non-stick frying pan. Put the slice of bread without cheese, oil side down, in the pan. Arrange the Emmental/Swiss cheese slices on top of the bread slice, then top with the beef and onions. Top with the processed-cheese-coated bread slice to enclose.

Turn the heat to medium and cook the first side for about 3–5 minutes until deep golden, pressing gently with a large spatula. Carefully turn with the spatula and cook on the other side, for 2–3 minutes more until deep golden brown all over.

Remove from the pan. Leave to cool for a few minutes before serving. Cut in half if sharing.

CHAPTER 6

LIVE LIFE ON THE VEG

Herbivores rejoice! Munch, crunch and lunch your way through this chapter, filled with freshness, flavour… and falafel. Whether you're after some pepper pizazz, zucchini zing or red onion razzmatazz, the Vegetable and Hummus Chapati Wrap, Courgette/Zucchini and Goats' Cheese Panini – and other offerings – will certainly deliver. Being healthy has never tasted so good.

Vegetable & Hummus
CHAPATI WRAPS

Wrap your lips around this delicious, nutritious flatbread filled with gratifying goodness. The simple Indian-style chapatis are given va-va-voom with raw, colourful, crunchy veggies and smooth, fluffy hummus. Go purist with a traditional flavour hummus or 'out there' with whatever variation takes your fancy – red (bell) pepper, sweet chilli/chile, caramelized onion, beetroot/beet… The recipe below makes six chapatis, so any left over can be frozen and reheated for another time. Give yourself a 'chapati' on the back for knocking up such a healthy, wholesome lunch.

2 chapati wraps (see below)

4 tablespoons your favourite hummus (for homemade, see page 9)

1 carrot

½ red, orange or yellow (bell) pepper, seeded and thinly sliced

handful watercress, rinsed

CHAPATI WRAPS

200 g/1½ cups wholemeal/whole-wheat flour (stone-ground if available), plus extra for dusting

pinch salt

MAKES 2

To make the chapati wraps, stir the flour together with the salt in a mixing bowl. Gradually mix in enough cold water (7–8 tablespoons) to give a soft but not sticky dough that comes together easily. Tip the dough out onto a lightly floured surface and knead for 4–5 minutes. Shape the dough into 6 balls and rest them under the upturned bowl for 30 minutes.

Dip each ball of dough in a little flour and roll out to a 20-cm/8-in. circle. Preheat a non-stick frying pan/skillet over medium-high heat. Add one chapati and cook for about 90 seconds, flipping over a couple of times, until the flatbread is patterned with brown spots and is cooked. Repeat with the remaining chapatis.

Use the chapati wraps while still warm or if they have cooled, gently warm them to make them more flexible, either by dry-frying for a few seconds each side in a frying pan, or in the microwave for 10 seconds on high.

Spread each wrap with hummus. Use a vegetable peeler to shave the carrot into ribbons, then divide these between the wraps. Add the pepper slices and watercress, roll up the wraps, and cut in half to serve.

COURGETTE, RED ONION & GOATS' CHEESE *Panini*

There are around 15 types of courgette/zucchini in the world, 20 varieties of onion and more than 1,800 kinds of cheese. Yes, really! Taking just three ingredients from this long and winding list – sprinkling in a touch of greenery – a winning combination of flavours can be found. By grilling the courgette, its taste is completely transformed, becoming sweeter and smokier. Add the creamy, dreamy goats' cheese and the satisfying crunch of the red onion, and you've got yourself a number-one sandwich.

1 ciabatta loaf

2 small courgettes/zucchinis, cut lengthways into slices 5 mm/¼ in. thick

8 thinly sliced rings red onion

1 tablespoon chopped fresh mint

2 handfuls rocket/arugula

100 g/3½ oz. firm goats' cheese, crumbled

olive oil, for brushing

salt and freshly ground black pepper

MAKES 2

Preheat a panini grill or ridged griddle/grill pan. Cut the top and bottom off the ciabatta, slice open lengthways and then cut in half.

Brush the courgette slices with a little oil and season with salt and pepper. Grill them for 1–2 minutes in the preheated panini grill or ridged griddle pan. Divide the courgette between the two sandwiches.

Top with the onions, mint and rocket, finishing with the cheese. Brush both sides of the panini with a little oil and toast in the panini grill or ridged griddle for 2–3 minutes. The bread should be golden brown and the filling warmed through. Serve immediately.

FALAFEL *Pitta Bread*

Fresh, filling and flavoursome, these Middle Eastern flatbreads will leave you feeling anything but flat. In fact, you'll feel positively elated as you bite down on the golden balls of deliciousness, drizzled with the nutty, lemony tarator sauce. With ancient origins in Egypt, the fantastic falafel could move mountains – or pyramids – with its distinctive flavour. Hot and crisp on the outside, herby and fluffy on the inside, it's fare fit for a King (Tut).

FALAFELS

500 ml/2¼ cups dried chickpeas

1 onion, quartered

2 teaspoons salt

freshly ground black pepper

2–3 garlic cloves

2–3 slices stale bread

3 tablespoons fresh flat-leaf parsley, finely chopped

⅓ red (bell) pepper

2 teaspoons ground cumin

2 teaspoons ground coriander

2 tablespoons plain/all-purpose flour

2 teaspoons baking powder

1 litre/quart vegetable oil, for deep-frying

TARATOR SAUCE (OPTIONAL)

175 ml/¾ cup tahini

freshly squeezed juice of 2 lemons

1 garlic clove, minced

1 teaspoon salt

handful fresh flat-leaf parsley, finely chopped, plus extra to serve

TO SERVE

8 pitta breads, toasted

cos/romaine lettuce

2 tomatoes, sliced

fresh mint leaves

salt and freshly ground black pepper

MAKES 8

Soak the chickpeas in a large bowl of cold water for at least 12 hours.

Drain the chickpeas and add to a food processor, along with the onion, salt, black pepper, garlic, bread, parsley, red pepper and ground cumin and coriander. Blend until it reaches a granular consistency. Add the flour, baking powder and 175 ml/¾ cup water and mix well.

Moisten your hands and form small balls of the chickpea mixture and flatten them slightly.

Heat the vegetable oil in a deep-fryer or a large frying pan/skillet to 190°C/375°F or until the oil is bubbling steadily. Fry the chickpea balls until golden brown. Remove the falafel and drain carefully using paper towels.

For the tarator sauce, if using, in a deep bowl, beat the tahini with the lemon juice and minced garlic until it becomes quite creamy. Add 175 ml/¾ cup water, little by little, and continue to beat well. Add the salt and parsley and stir. Taste and if the sauce isn't tangy enough, add a little bit more lemon juice. Refrigerate until ready to use.

To serve, stuff a couple of lettuce leaves into each pitta bread and add a few falafel, the tomato slices, parsley, mint and some salt and pepper. Drizzle over the sauce and serve.

Caprese PANINI

Say 'ciao bella' to this juicy, oozy melt, which waves the Italian flag with its vibrant colours. Taking its name from the island of Capri in the Bay of Naples, Caprese is commonly eaten as a salad, but the simple components of ripe tomatoes, creamy mozzarella and sweet basil also work beautifully in a panini. The key to mouthwatering success lies solely with the quality of the ingredients – don't you dare scrimp. Mamma mia (*chef's kiss*).

2 ciabatta rolls

2 ripe tomatoes, sliced

150 g/5 oz. mozzarella cheese, sliced

8 fresh basil leaves

olive oil, for brushing

freshly ground black pepper

MAKES 2

Cut the rolls in half. Lightly brush the insides with olive oil. Layer the tomato, mozzarella and basil leaves and season with black pepper. Add the top halves of the bread and brush the outsides with olive oil.

Heat a panini press. Cook the sandwiches until the cheese has melted and the bread has turned golden. If you don't have a panini press, use a ridged griddle/grill pan over medium-high heat instead, weighing the sandwiches down with a heavy pan while toasting. Flip the sandwiches halfway through cooking. Serve immediately.

Egg Salad
SANDWICH

Nobody wants egg on their face. Unless they're getting stuck into an Egg Salad Sandwich, then it's perfectly acceptable – embraced even – to require a napkin to wipe a little egg from the sides of your mouth. To add a little zing, this recipe calls for lemon zest, but you can use any number of things to jazz up the simple sandwich: chopped celery for crunch, avocado for extra creaminess, mustard for added tang… Use your imagination, then stuff your face.

butter, at room temperature

4 slices white or wholemeal bread

4 lettuce leaves

2 tablespoons mayonnaise (see page 8)

½ teaspoon grated lemon zest

2 hard-boiled eggs, cooled, peeled and chopped

salt and freshly ground black pepper

MAKES 2

Thinly butter the bread. Lay a lettuce leaf on top of 2 slices.

Combine the mayonnaise and lemon zest, then season with salt and black pepper. Add the hard-boiled eggs and fold together. Divide the mixture evenly on top of the lettuce.

Top with another lettuce leaf and the remaining slices of buttered bread. Cut in half and serve.

CUCUMBER
Sandwich

Described in Oscar Wilde's *The Importance of Being Earnest* as a 'reckless extravagance', Cucumber Sandwiches have long been associated with the upper crust of society. These days, they're still fancy but are accessible to all – indeed, no afternoon tea, garden party or baby shower would be complete without them. Dainty, refreshing and quintessentially English, they are the perfect accompaniment to a cup of tea (pinkies up) or pitcher of Pimm's. Meet you on the croquet lawn.

¼ cucumber, thinly sliced

4 slices white bread
(the softer the better)

2 tablespoons cream cheese,
at room temperature

chives, watercress, dill,
mint leaves or lemon zest
(optional)

salt and ground white
or black pepper

MAKES 8

To avoid any sogginess, salt the cucumber first (the salt will draw some of the liquid out and make the slices firmer). Line a chopping board with paper towels and spread the cucumber slices on top. Sprinkle lightly with salt and leave for 20 minutes. Pat dry with paper towels.

Lay the slices of bread on a different chopping board and spread one side of each slice with cream cheese. Arrange the cucumber on two of the slices and sprinkle with pepper and any of the optional ingredients, if using. Close the sandwiches with the other bread slices. Chop the crusts off, and then cut into triangles. Serve immediately.

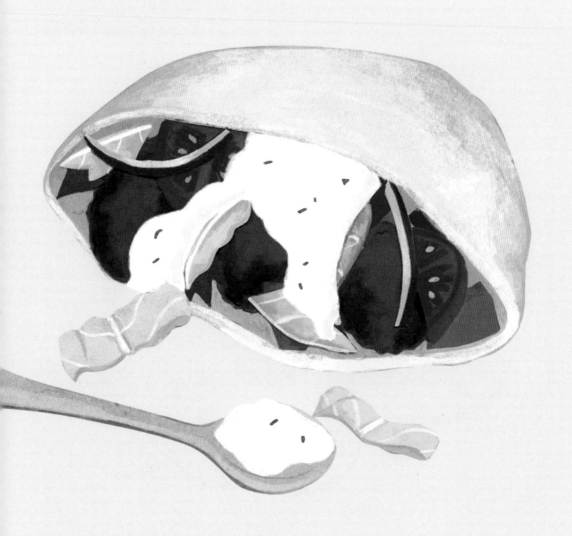

CHAPTER 7

SUMMER TREATS

Swing open the patio doors and hit the garden… Grab
a picnic blanket and head to the park… Find a bench with
a view and watch the sunset… How will you be dining alfresco
this summer? Get your fill of fresh air while filling up on
Mother-Nature-approved delights – think Lamb Kofta Pittas,
Chicken Caesar Wraps and Ice Cream Sandwiches. When it
comes to summer snacking, you'll have it licked.

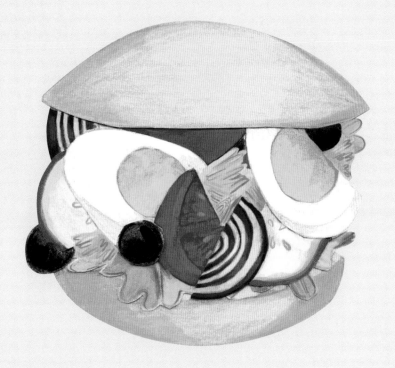

Picnic LOAF

Who needs a picnic hamper when you've got a picnic loaf? With so many ingredients layered up, you won't require any more to fill your tummy as you dine alfresco at the park (don't forget the picnic blanket). While lesser sandwiches may get squashed en route, this robust mega-roll holds its own while holding its shape. Make sure you get your jaw in training, though, as the chunky cob requires some serious bite. Chomp!

1 red (bell) pepper, deseeded and quartered

1 yellow (bell) pepper, deseeded and quartered

2 courgettes/zucchini, sliced lengthways

1 aubergine/eggplant, sliced lengthways

1 garlic clove, crushed

1 white cob loaf

2 balls mozzarella cheese

3–4 tablespoons pesto (see page 7) or black olive tapenade (see page 9)

fresh basil leaves

8 semi-dried/sun-blush tomatoes, chopped

10 slices salami

olive oil, for roasting

salt and freshly ground black pepper

MAKES 1 (SERVES 6)

Preheat the oven to 180°C/350°F/Gas 4. Mix all the vegetables with the crushed garlic and a glug of olive oil, then season with salt and pepper. Lay them in a roasting pan, without overlapping. Roast for 25–30 minutes, turning once. Set aside to cool in the pan.

Cut off the top third of the loaf to make a lid. Using your hands, hollow out the inside of the loaf by pulling out most of the bread. Make sure to leave a 3-cm/1¼-in. crust around the outside; any thinner and the moisture from the vegetables will turn the crust soggy.

Drain the mozzarella and slice it. Spread the pesto or tapenade around the inside of the loaf, then layer all the ingredients on top. Put the lid back on when the loaf is full and wrap the whole thing tightly in clingfilm/plastic wrap. Weigh the loaf down with something heavy on top. If possible, leave to press for a few hours at room temperature.

To serve, remove the clingfilm and cut the loaf into wedges.

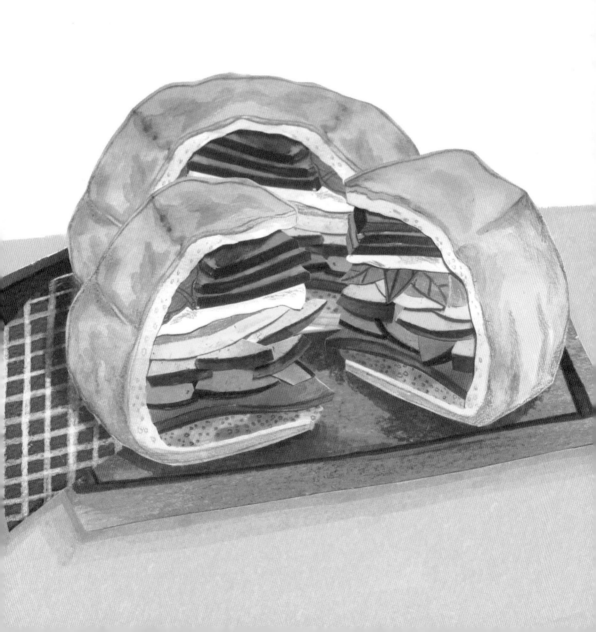

Chicken Caesar
SALAD WRAP

All hail the Chicken Caesar Salad Wrap. Adapted from the classic Caesar salad, which was created by Italian restaurateur Caesar Cardini in Mexico in 1924, the original recipe called for a squeeze of lime juice. Now, it's all about the lemon. The garlicky, mustardy, salty, lemony combination of flavours have become so popular that McDonald's even invented the Caesar Chicken McWrap. If you're a fan of the salad and think you'll miss the crunch of the croutons, you could always sneak a few inside your wrap. I came, I saw, I devoured.

75 g/2¾ oz. Parmesan cheese

4 tortilla wraps

8–12 cos/romaine lettuce leaves, depending on size

300 g/10½ oz. cooked skinless chicken fillets, sliced

CAESAR DRESSING

2 garlic cloves, crushed

2 anchovy fillets in oil, drained and chopped

1 egg yolk

1 tablespoon white wine vinegar

1 tablespoon Dijon mustard

freshly squeezed juice of ½ lemon

60 ml/¼ cup light olive oil

60 ml/¼ cup sunflower oil

freshly ground black pepper

MAKES 4

To prepare the Caesar dressing, mash the garlic and anchovies to a paste in a small bowl. Put in a food processor with the egg yolk, vinegar, mustard, lemon juice and a little black pepper. Blend together briefly, then, with the motor still running, add the oils in a slow trickle through the feed tube.

Use a potato peeler to make Parmesan cheese shavings. Lay the tortilla wraps out on a clean work surface and top each one with 2–3 lettuce leaves, a few chicken breast slices and some Parmesan shavings. Drizzle with Caesar dressing.

Roll each wrap tightly, cut in half diagonally and serve.

Lamb Kofta PITTA

Spicy, flavoursome meat? *Check!* Fresh, minty sauce? *Check!* Delightful, fragrant lemongrass skewers? *Check!* Seasoned with herbs and spices, then fried to perfection and nestled inside warm bread with crunchy veggies, lamb koftas are popular in many countries, including Tunisia, Morocco, Greece, Turkey and India. If you'd rather not use lemongrass skewers, you can use pre-soaked wooden or bamboo cocktail sticks/toothpicks instead.

3 lemongrass stalks

200 g/7 oz. minced/ground lamb

2 shallots, finely chopped

2 teaspoons chopped fresh parsley

2 teaspoons chopped fresh coriander/cilantro

½ teaspoon ground allspice

1 small red chilli/chile, deseeded and finely chopped

flour, for dusting

2 tablespoons sunflower oil

½ small red (bell) pepper, deseeded and cut into thin strips

12 white mini pittas, warmed

12 crisp baby lettuce leaves

16 cherry tomatoes, halved

1 red onion, finely sliced

12 small sprigs fresh coriander/cilantro

MINTED CRÈME FRAÎCHE

125 ml/½ cup half-fat crème fraîche

2 tablespoons chopped fresh mint

salt and freshly ground black pepper

MAKES 12 (SERVES 4)

Slice the lemongrass in half widthways, then lengthways to make 12 sticks. In a bowl, mix the minced lamb, shallots, parsley, coriander, allspice and chilli together. Divide into 12 and, with lightly floured hands, shape into 5-cm/2-in. long finger shapes. Thread the koftas onto the lemongrass skewers.

In a small bowl, mix the crème fraîche and mint together and season with salt and pepper.

Heat the oil in a frying pan/skillet and fry the koftas for 4–5 minutes, turning to brown on all sides. At the same time, add the pepper strips and cook for 3–4 minutes to soften and brown slightly.

Open each pitta bread lengthways, place a lettuce leaf in each and add a kofta, a few strips of red pepper, some tomatoes, red onion and a sprig of coriander. Serve the wraps with the minted crème fraîche.

PAN BAGNAT

A salad Niçoise in sandwich form, the translation of 'Pan Bagnat' is 'bathed bread'. It's the ultimate make-ahead feast – leave it chilling in the fridge to allow the juices, oils and flavours to soak sumptuously into the bread. A speciality of Nice in the sunny South of France, it can be found in pretty much every boulangerie, market, cafe, bistro and beach stand in the area. A Mediterranean meal of mammoth proportions.

285 g/10 oz. canned tuna fish packed in oil

30 g/¼ cup pitted/stoned black olives

2 anchovy fillets, finely chopped

1–2 tablespoons red wine vinegar

2 crusty bread rolls

1 garlic clove, crushed

60 ml/¼ cup olive oil

handful baby leaf lettuce leaves

½ small red onion, thinly sliced

2 hard-boiled eggs, sliced

2 tomatoes, sliced

¼ cucumber, sliced

salt and freshly ground black pepper

MAKES 2

Combine the tuna and its oil with the olives, anchovies and 2 teaspoons of the red wine vinegar. Stir gently, ensuring you keep the tuna 'chunky'.

Slice the rolls in half and remove some of the bread inside to make room for the filling. In a small bowl, mix the garlic, olive oil, salt, pepper and the rest of the red wine vinegar together. Brush this inside both the top and bottom of the rolls.

Divide the tuna mixture between the bread rolls, then top with the lettuce, red onion, egg, tomato and cucumber. Close the sandwiches and wrap them tightly – separately – in clingfilm/plastic wrap.

Place them next to each other on a work surface and put a chopping board on top. Weigh down with something heavy like a pot or a few cans. Press the sandwiches for 10 minutes on one side, then turn them over and press on the other side for another 10 minutes.

Still wrapped, place in the fridge for up to 24 hours, then remove and let the sandwiches warm to room temperature, before serving.

ICE CREAM *Sandwich*

Here's the scoop: these sweet treats will melt away any stresses of your day. You'll be catapulted back to your childhood as you bite, lick and drip your way through this nostalgic nom-nom. Swap the peanuts for any other type of nut if you fancy – walnuts and pecans work well. And mix things up with different ice cream flavours too.

175 g/1½ sticks butter, soft and cubed

75 g/⅓ cup peanut butter

175 g/¾ cup plus 2 tablespoons packed light brown soft sugar

75 g/⅓ cup golden caster/superfine sugar

1 egg and 1 egg yolk, beaten

1 teaspoon pure vanilla extract

225 g/1⅔ cups plain/all-purpose flour

1 teaspoon bicarbonate of/baking soda

½ teaspoon baking powder

pinch salt

75 g/½ cup salted roasted peanuts, roughly chopped

150 g/1 cup chocolate chips (milk or dark/semisweet)

about 10 scoops good-quality vanilla or chocolate ice cream, slightly softened

baking sheet, lined with parchment paper

MAKES ABOUT 20

Put the butter, peanut butter and sugars into the bowl of a stand mixer (or use a handheld mixer) and beat until light and creamy. Add the beaten egg to the creamed mixture in 3 batches, mixing well between each addition. Add the vanilla and mix again.

Sift the flour, bicarbonate of soda, baking powder and salt into the bowl and mix to just combine. Add the peanuts and chocolate chips and mix again until thoroughly combined. Wrap the dough in clingfilm/plastic wrap and refrigerate for at least 2 hours.

Preheat the oven to 170°C/325°F/Gas 3.

Roll the dough into balls no bigger than a walnut and arrange on the lined baking sheet, spacing them well apart. Slightly flatten each ball of dough with your hand and bake in batches for about 10–12 minutes, or until golden. Remove from the oven and allow to cool on the baking sheets for 3–4 minutes, then transfer to a wire rack and allow to cool completely.

To serve, lay half of the cookies on the work surface, flat-side up. Top with a scoop of ice cream and sandwich together with another cookie. Eat immediately.

If you don't want to use all the cookies in one go, freeze some. After they are completely cooled, place in a single layer on a lined baking sheet and put in the freezer. When the cookies are frozen, place in a freezer bag, squeezing out any excess air. Store flat in the freezer. When you want to use them, defrost at room temperature and then add the ice cream filling.

CHAPTER 8

GO BIG OR
GO HOME

Dainty diners look away now. This chapter requires big appetites, big bites… and big buns. A colossal Club Sandwich, mountainous Muffaletta and hefty Hoagie are all on the menu, as are other towering treats. Indulge in these superhero sandwiches and you'll never be hungry again… well, at least not until dinnertime. Is your jaw ready?

Club SANDWICH

Hungry? Join the club! There's debate as to where the Club Sandwich originated but many believe it was at New York City's oldest private members' society The Union Club. This prestigious establishment – complete with grand piano, chandeliers and more money than you can shake a cocktail stick at – opened its Gucci-clad arms to the likes of Dwight D. Eisenhower, J. P. Morgan and James Gordon Bennett Jr., who inspired the British exclamation 'Gordon Bennett!'. The Union Club is still going strong today – time to dig out a jacket as you dig into this once-fancy-pants fare.

12 slices sourdough bread

2 avocados

8 cos/romaine lettuce leaves, finely chopped

175 g/¾ cup mayonnaise (see page 8) or Dijonnaise

3 large tomatoes, cut into 16 thick slices

16 slices bacon

8 slices roasted turkey breast

16 slices cured ham

8 slices fontina cheese

salt and freshly ground black pepper

cocktail sticks/toothpicks

MAKES 4

Toast the bread in a toaster or under a grill/broiler on both sides. Pit/stone, peel and slice the avocados. Arrange the finely chopped lettuce into 8 stacks.

Arrange 4 bread slices in a row. Spread 1 tablespoon of mayonnaise or Dijonnaise over 1 side of each slice of bread. Place a lettuce stack on the top of the first slice of bread. Top with 2 tomato slices, a few slices of avocado and season with salt and pepper if needed. Place 2 slices of bacon on top, then a slice of turkey, 2 slices of ham and a slice of the cheese. Season with salt and pepper. Place the second bread slice on top and repeat the layering. Spread 1 tablespoon mayonnaise or Dijonnaise over the final 4 slices and add these to the tops of the sandwiches, mayonnaise/Dijonnaise-side down.

Pin each sandwich together by piercing it with cocktail sticks/toothpicks to secure.

MUFFALETTA

The vibrant city of New Orleans is famous for its world-class jazz clubs, parties in the street, Creole architecture… and the mighty Muffaletta sandwich. Invented by a Sicilian immigrant deli owner in 1906, it's a sandwich packed with so much panache, it'll be like Mardi Gras in your mouth. Not for little nibblers, the layers upon layers of cheese, meat, salad and other good stuff will satisfy even the most ravenous of revellers.

4 large baps/buns

butter, at room temperature

200 g/7 oz. your favourite sliced cheese

200 g/7 oz. tomatoes, sliced

8 tablespoons black olive paste (see page 9)

1 red onion, sliced in thin rings

4 slices Parma ham

8 slices chorizo or salami

350 g/12 oz. freshly cooked chicken, pulled into strips

4 teaspoons Dijon mustard (optional)

4 tablespoons mayonnaise (see page 8)

MAKES 4

Halve the baps and spread with butter and some of the black olive paste. Layer up the rest of the ingredients as liked.

Dot with mustard (or spread the other half of the bap with it), if using. Add blobs of mayonnaise. Spread some more black olive paste on the other half of the bap. Put the top of the bap in place and press closed. Serve immediately.

CEMITA

Set your taste buds into a Mexican wave with this overflowing burger-like beauty that hails from Puebla in Mexico. You'll want to rejoice as you sink your teeth into the crunchy crust of the bread, golden meat cutlet, ripe avocado, skinny strands of cheese and other intoxicating components. The combined textures are oh-so tantalizing. Some of the ingredients – such as the Oaxaca cheese, papalo herb and cemita itself (which refers to the plain bread roll as well as the full sandwich) may be tricky to come by outside of Mexico, but, fret not, decent alternatives are available (in brackets below).

1 large/US extra large egg, beaten

125 g/1 cup breadcrumbs

4 x 170-g/6-oz. pork, chicken or beef cutlets, very thinly pounded

2 avocados, peeled, stoned/pitted and sliced

4 cemita (or sesame seed) buns

250 g/2 cups queso Oaxaca (or mozzarella, Monterey jack or string cheese), shredded

12 slices onion, about 5 mm/¼ in. thick

4 chipotle chillies/chiles or pickled jalapeño peppers, chopped

20 papalo (or fresh coriander/cilantro) leaves

vegetable oil, for frying

salt and freshly ground black pepper

MAKES 4

Place the beaten egg and breadcrumbs in two separate shallow dishes. One at a time, dip each cutlet in the egg first, then the breadcrumbs, making sure the meat is fully covered.

Pour about 1 cm/½ in. of vegetable oil in a frying pan/skillet and place over high heat. In batches, fry the cutlets for about 3 minutes on each side, turning once, until golden brown (add oil as needed to maintain the level). Transfer to a plate with paper towels on and season with salt and pepper.

Halve the buns and place the avocado on the bottom halves. Top with the fried cutlets and pile half the cheese on top. Arrange the onion slices on top of the cheese, then add the chipotle or jalapeño pieces. Top with papalo or coriander and mound the remaining cheese on top.

As the buns are jam-packed, create space by scooping some bread out from each of the 'lids'. Close and serve right away.

FRANCESINHA

Channel your inner caveman as you rip apart the meat layered on meat layered on meat inside this mega mountain of a meal. Literally translated as 'little French girl', there's nothing little about the Francesinha, which hails from Porto in Portugal. Originally adapted from the classier Croque Monsieur, the tomato and beer sauce liberally poured on top is a very welcome addition. Serve with French fries and prepare to get saucy.

2 thin steaks

2 sausages

8 slices Cheddar cheese

4 slices thick white bread

4 slices ham or salami

2 eggs (optional)

SAUCE

2 small onions, chopped

4 garlic cloves, crushed

55 g/3½ tablespoons butter

2 tablespoons olive oil

2 bay leaves

500 ml/2 cups tomato passata/strained tomatoes

1 fresh chilli/chile or pinch chilli flakes/hot red pepper flakes

330 ml/1½ cups beer

500 ml/2 cups beef or chicken stock

2 tablespoons milk

2 tablespoons plain/all-purpose flour

salt and freshly ground black pepper

MAKES 2

Season the steaks and sausages with salt and pepper. Cut the sausages lengthways and cook them under the grill/broiler or in a ridged griddle/grill pan until cooked through, reserving the fat they drip. Grill the steaks to how you like them cooked.

To make the sauce, sizzle the onions and garlic in a pan with the butter, olive oil, bay leaves and sausage fat. Add the passata and chilli, then bring to the boil. Add the beer and stock, and simmer for 10–20 minutes. Mix the milk and flour together with a fork, and add it to the sauce to thicken it, as necessary. Remove the bay leaves and whizz with a hand-held blender until smooth.

To assemble the sandwiches, place a slice of cheese on a slice of bread, then layer the steak, sausages and ham/salami. Place another slice of bread on top. Repeat to make the second sandwich. Cover both with the remaining cheese. Put in the oven or under the grill/broiler until the cheese has melted.

If you are opting for eggs, fry them both and place one on top of each sandwich. Pour the sauce over.

HOAGIE

Be warned: this is a mayonnaise-free zone. While the creamy condiment is used – often in abundance – in many a sandwich, a true hoagie only calls for oil and vinegar from the condiment tray. The name hoagie likely comes from Philadelphia's Hog Island, where Italian immigrants worked in the shipyard during World War I and would make sandwiches filled with meat, cheese and salad. They were called 'Hoggies', later to become 'Hoagies'. One bite and you'll be in hog heaven.

1 hoagie/sub roll

2 teaspoons olive oil

1½ teaspoons red wine vinegar

¾ teaspoon dried oregano

3 slices ham

3 slices Genoa salami

3 slices provolone cheese

½ tomato, sliced

⅛ red onion, thinly sliced

handful lettuce leaves of your choice

salt and freshly ground black pepper

MAKES 1

Slice the roll lengthways. Brush the inside with 1 teaspoon of the olive oil and ½ teaspoon of the vinegar. Sprinkle a bit of salt and ¼ teaspoon of the oregano on top.

Layer the ingredients – first the ham, then the salami, cheese, tomato, onion and lettuce. Drizzle the remaining oil and vinegar over the length of the lettuce. Sprinkle a little salt and pepper, and the rest of the oregano. Cut the sandwich in half to make it easier to eat.

Pulled Pork BAPS

Eat high on the hog with these tender, melt-in-the-mouth munches. If you're into instant gratification, turn the page now. This recipe requires many, many hours of slow-cooking in order to get the pork pull-worthy and juuuuust right. But as you sink your teeth into this sublime sandwich – relishing the contrast of the soft, fluffy bread; succulent, juicy meat; and crunchy, creamy coleslaw – you'll realise it's oh-so worth the wait.

2 onions, thinly sliced

4 garlic cloves, thinly sliced

120 ml/½ cup apple cider vinegar

120 ml/½ cup India pale ale (IPA)

1 fresh sage leaf

1 tablespoon packed dark brown sugar

1 tablespoon chilli/chili powder

1 tablespoon salt, plus more as needed

1 teaspoon freshly ground black pepper

½ teaspoon ground cumin

¼ teaspoon ground cinnamon

2.25-kg/5-lb. boneless or bone-in pork shoulder, twine or netting removed

450 g/2 cups barbeque sauce (optional)

6 baps

butter, at room temperature

coleslaw (optional)

MAKES 6

Place the onions and garlic in an even layer in a slow cooker, pour in the vinegar and beer and add the sage leaf.

Combine the sugar, chilli powder, salt, pepper, cumin and cinnamon in a small bowl. Pat the pork dry with paper towels. Rub the spice mixture all over the pork and place the meat on top of the onions and garlic. Cover and cook until the pork is fork-tender, about 6–8 hours on a high setting or 8–10 hours on low.

Turn off the slow cooker and move the pork to a cutting board. Set a fine-mesh sieve/strainer over a medium-sized heatproof bowl. Pour the onion mixture from the slow cooker through the sieve/strainer and return the solids to the slow cooker. Set the strained liquid aside and use a spoon to skim and discard any fat from the surface.

If the pork has a bone, remove and discard it. Using 2 forks, shred the pork, discarding any large pieces of fat. Return the shredded meat to the slow cooker and add the barbeque sauce, if using, and mix to combine. Add 60 ml/¼ cup of the strained liquid at a time to the slow cooker until the pork is just moistened. Taste and season with salt as needed.

Cut each bap in half and butter the bottom. Lay a generous helping of pork onto each bun, spoon over the sauce and top with coleslaw, if using.

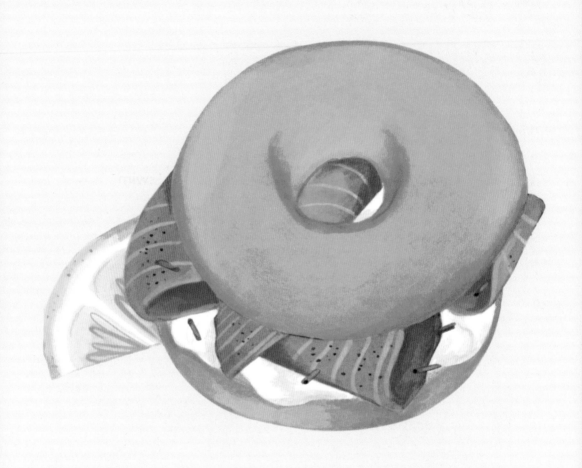

CHAPTER 9

A DIFFERENT KETTLE OF FISH

Get your dose of Vitamin Sea. From the no-fuss Fish Finger Sandwich to the sophisticated Salmon and Cream Cheese Bagel, the recipes in this chapter positively swim with flavour. Whether you've got a hankering for breaded prawns/shrimp, lobster, cod or mackerel, the Po'Boy, Lobster Roll and Fischbrötchen will oblige. Dive in!

PO' Boy

Rich in flavour, this Louisiana classic was created by two streetcar conductors in 1929, who would feed striking workers – stating, 'Here comes another poor boy', before handing over their hearty, affordable fare. The sandwiches became known as 'Poor Boys' themselves, later 'Po' Boys'. The filling varies, with roast beef being popular, or some kind of fried seafood like prawns/shrimp, crawfish, oysters or crab. Teamed with a ridiculously remarkable tangy mayonnaise, boy, are they tasty!

100 g/1 cup plain/all-purpose flour

2 tablespoons Cajun seasoning

100 g/1 cup dried breadcrumbs

200 g/7 oz. raw king prawns/jumbo shrimp, peeled

2 eggs, beaten

sunflower oil, for frying

2 small baguettes

handful shredded iceberg lettuce

2 tomatoes, sliced

TANGY MAYONNAISE

2 tablespoons mayonnaise (see page 8)

½ garlic clove, crushed

1 tablespoon Dijon mustard

½ teaspoon paprika

few drops Tabasco sauce

salt and freshly ground black pepper

MAKES 2

Mix the mayonnaise ingredients together in a bowl and season well with salt and pepper.

Combine the flour with half the Cajun seasoning on a plate. Mix the breadcrumbs with the rest of the Cajun seasoning on a different plate.

Dip the prawns in the flour mix first, then in the egg, then in the breadcrumb mix. Pour 2.5 cm/1 in. of oil in a large frying pan/skillet and heat. Cook the prawns for about a minute on each side until golden. Drain on paper towels.

Cut the baguettes in half lengthways. Spread the mayonnaise inside – if there's any left over, serve on the side. Lay the prawns on top, followed by the lettuce and tomato slices. Close the baguettes, cut in half and serve.

Lobster ROLL

Pinch me. This dreamy dish inspires fantasies of salty sea breezes and lazy, hazy days sitting on the dock of the bay. Instead of watching the tide roll away, however, you can watch your lobster roll head towards your eager lips. A dish native to New England in the US, it's a Maine attraction for tourists and locals alike, all wanting to get their claws into this fresh, flavourful feast that captures summertime in a bun.

500 g/1 lb. 2 oz. cooked lobster

2 celery stalks, diced

5 tablespoons mayonnaise (see page 8)

1 tablespoon freshly squeezed lemon juice

small pinch ground cayenne pepper

6 hot dog or brioche buns

1 tablespoon butter

freshly ground black pepper

crisps/potato chips, to serve

MAKES 6

Carefully crack the lobsters open – or ask your fishmonger to remove the shells. Pull out the lobster meat and chop it roughly into chunks. Put in a bowl, cover and chill.

Mix the celery, mayonnaise, lemon juice and cayenne together. Season with black pepper, then taste. Add more lemon juice if needed. Toss the lobster with the mixture.

Slice each bun open (on the top rather than the side), being careful not to cut all the way through. Melt the butter in a frying pan/skillet. Fry the rolls for 1–2 minutes on the cut sides until golden. Pile the lobster filling into rolls, and serve with ready salted crisps/potato chips.

Salmon & Cream Cheese
BAGEL

A delicate deli delicacy (what a mouthful!), make sure you slather on lashings of cream cheese and layer the salmon liberally for an extra-indulgent treat. Similar to the 'lox and schmear' bagel enjoyed in American Jewish communities, the Salmon and Cream Cheese Bagel is a popular breakfast or brunch offering. Add capers for a salty tang or chives for an oniony nod. A sumptuous sandwich that really fills a hole.

2 bagels

100 g/3½ oz. cream cheese

125 g/4½ oz. smoked salmon slices

capers (optional)

chives, snipped (optional)

lemon wedges

freshly ground black pepper

MAKES 2

Split the bagels in half horizontally and toast on both sides in a toaster, under the grill/broiler or using a stove-top grill pan.

Spread the bottom half of each bagel with cream cheese and fold the slices of smoked salmon on top. Add the capers, if using, and squeeze over plenty of lemon juice. Grind some black pepper over and sprinkle with snipped chives, if you desire. Serve topped with the second half of the bagels.

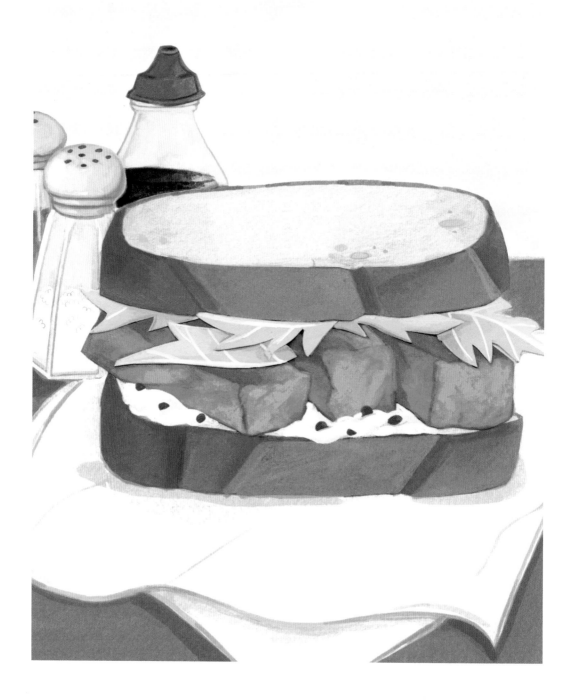

FISH FINGER *Sandwich*

Like strawberries and cream at Wimbledon, roast dinner in the pub and talking about the weather, Fish Finger Sandwiches have become somewhat of a British institution. Gone are the days when breaded fish fingers/fish sticks meant a quick after-school dinner when your mum was too tired to cook; now, top chefs are whipping up posh fish finger dishes with aplomb. You can do the same with this crunchy, flaky, tangy sandwich – complete with homemade tartare sauce. One chomp and you'll be hooked.

2 fillets of cod or haddock, skinned and boned

sunflower or vegetable oil

4 slices white bread

butter, at room temperature

4 tablespoons Tartare Sauce (see page 7)

handful lettuce leaves of your choice

BEER BATTER

200 g/1½ cups plain/ all-purpose flour

2 teaspoons salt

2 x 330-ml/11-fl. oz. bottles of lager

MAKES 2

Slice the fish into 6 finger-size strips.

For the batter, whisk the flour, salt and lager in a bowl until combined. Fill a large frying pan/skillet with about 2.5 cm/ 1 in. oil over high heat (don't leave it unattended). When the oil is bubbling steadily, it's ready. Dip the fish fingers in the batter, remove any excess and then lower carefully into the oil, using tongs if necessary. Fry for about 4 minutes on each side over moderate heat until golden and crispy.

Remove the fish fingers carefully from the oil and drain on paper towels. Season with salt.

Butter 2 slices of bread, before spreading a couple of tablespoons of tartare sauce on. Place 3 fish fingers on top of each one, add lettuce, then close the sandwiches with the other slices of bread. Serve warm.

FISCHBRÖTCHEN

Holy mackerel! Something extremely fishy is going on. The buttery, flaky star of this sandwich will certainly make a splash inside your mouth, while the velvety-yet-crunchy remoulade sauce is off-the-scales scrummy. Commonly eaten in northern Germany, the Fischbrötchen isn't strict on which fish to fill(et) the roll with – herring, salmon, cod and mackerel are popular choices, with prawn/shrimp or breaded fishcakes sometimes making an appearance. Whatever you go for, the combination of flavours is sure to reel you in.

2 tablespoons butter

2 fillets cod, herring, salmon or mackerel

2 bread rolls

2 large leaves butterhead lettuce

few slices red onion

pickle slices (optional)

REMOULADE

400 g/14 oz. mayonnaise (see page 8)

1 egg, hard-boiled and chopped into small pieces

1 small onion, finely chopped

1 tablespoon capers, finely chopped

3 cornichons, finely chopped

handful fresh parsley, finely chopped

handful fresh dill, finely chopped

splash of cornichon liquid

salt and freshly ground black pepper

MAKES 2

To make the remoulade, mix the mayonnaise, egg, onion, capers, cornichons and herbs together. Add a splash of cornichon liquid and stir, then season. If there's time, refrigerate for a few hours to allow the flavours to blend.

Heat the butter in a frying pan/skillet over medium heat and cook the fish for 4–5 minutes on each side (adjust as necessary according to the thickness). Transfer to a plate lined with a paper towel.

Cut the bread rolls in half. Spread the remoulade on the bottom, then add the lettuce, fish, red onion and pickle slices, if using. Serve the remaining remoulade on the side.